PRAISE FOR *AFTER*

"When one is working at the highest realms of the imagination and poetic craft, there is a curious sense in which the activities of writing, translating, even reading, and editing, are less distinct than we might think, that they are rather modes of the human mind's central creative enterprise. The poems in *After* reach these realms; over and over they evince that the highest poetic intelligence may not be originality but attentiveness and conversation. Long recognized as one of our finest translators, *After* is the book that will convince you that Geoffrey Brock is undoubtedly one of our finest poets as well. I will be reading and returning to these poems for the rest of my life."

—**Jennifer Grotz, author of *Still Falling***

"Although Geoff Brock's new collection has much to say about aging and loss, the intricate variations he plays on these themes lend his poems an unexpectedly celebratory air—an air of joyous discovery. To weave together two of his indelible images, the evening that reaches for our ripening fingers is always brightened by 'the old moon on its nightly walk, / the belled stars chiming faintly in their dark.' Few poets working today are as inventive as Brock in their use of meter and rhyme, and none makes the demotic speech of our era feel quite so numinous. Like Frost before him, Brock has the power to make earthbound words take flight."

—**Boris Dralyuk, author of *My Hollywood and Other Poems***

"To read Geoffrey Brock's *After* is to be in intimate conversation with poets he has loved—Pavese, Keats, Heaney (to name a few) and most importantly, the poet's father, Van K. Brock. As such, these poems braid 'some old-world air' with 'some brave new word.' The poems in *After* crackle and burst, unfolding with quiet authority, with wind and wisdom, nodding both to formalism and the vernacular. Brock gives us an almanac of seeing (and yes, feeling) from the middle of a life—a testament of loss and wonder and going on by a poet whose ear is pitch-perfect and whose singular voice is measured, monumental—and not to be missed."

—Andrea Cohen, author of *The Sorrow Apartments*

"*After* is a work of expert design, allusion, and rigor at the blurred edges, a book that lays bare the betrayals and 'gray sins' of a grievous, fragile life. An unnervingly casual master of the line and image—a herd of cattle is 'like ink in a bottle'; the Turin sky is 'rinsed with milk, clear but not luminous'—Brock has a wry, lacerating self-awareness that reminds me of Edgar Bowers. This is an elegiac, elemental, exquisite book."

—Randall Mann, author of *Deal: New and Selected Poems*

AFTER

for Sierra,
well met in SLO!

AFTER

POEMS

Geoffrey Brock

PAUL DRY BOOKS
Philadelphia 2024

First Paul Dry Books Edition, 2024

Paul Dry Books, Inc.
Philadelphia, Pennsylvania
www.pauldrybooks.com

Printed in the United States of America

Library of Congress Control Number: 2023952090

ISBN 978-1-58988-187-7

Dangerous pavements.
But this year I face the ice
with my father's stick.

—*Seamus Heaney*

CONTENTS

III

AFTER

THE DAY

It hangs on its
        stem like a plum
at the edge of a
        darkening thicket.

It's swelling and
        blushing and ripe
and I reach out a
        hand to pick it

but flesh moves
        slow through time
and evening
        comes on fast

and just when I
        think my fingers
might seize that
        sweetness at last

the gentlest of
        breezes rises
and the plum lets
        go of the stem.

And now it's my
        fingers ripening
and evening that's
        reaching for them.

ANNUNCIATION

The doctor enters, an angel
in teal, lifting

her eyes and leaning
toward my father to speak,

~~an olive branch in her pale hand~~

a stethoscope
draped on a clipboard

in her pale hand.
Her voice becomes

a torrent of light, an interior
wind. My father, in bed,

tries to turn away.
Between and above them,

~~a gold dove hovers and glows~~

a drip bag, backlit,
hovers and glows.

Monitors chirp.
Flocks of words fly

from the book that lies
half-open on my lap.

FORCES OF NATURE

This autumn morning, after the freeze,
They held a summit of the trees.
Motions were made and seconded,
And all the ochre, brown, and red
Snowed down. Each ruined crown agrees:
Today is a day for obsequies.
And since the colors haven't bled,
Our hill is a map of colonies
       This autumn morning:

Ochre, the land of the hackberries;
Red, of the maple—geographies
That spur my daughter to grab her sled
And raise those nations of the dead,
Scorning and smearing their boundaries
       This autumn morning.

GEOFFREY BROCK

STREET VIEW (A VISITATION)

He still drops in occasionally on my dreams
with pointless scraps of news from the afterlife,
so when the image of his old house loaded
and there he stood, loitering like a ghost
in the front yard, it wasn't a total shock.
His back is turned, so Google hasn't had
(I'm oddly grateful for this) to blur his face.
He stands between his mailbox and a newly
transplanted dogwood whose white flowers seem
too big for its thin trunk. It's spring: the redbud
is blooming too and the oak is leafing out
with that unspeakably bright chartreuse of April.
His left hand rests on his hip, his right is clutching
mail he must just have taken from the box.

He's likely thinking of something quite mundane
(lawn care, I'd guess), but somehow the tableau—
he's dressed in white, his head is slightly bowed—
puts me in mind of an aging, wingless Gabriel
reliving his famous scene, recalling his lines,
perhaps, or the odd look on Mary's face.
The photo, Google says, is five years old:
he's 81, has three years left. If it's Friday,
we'll all be joining him, in an hour or two,
for pizza. He'll have cleared his sprawl of papers
from the dining table to make room for us,
there'll be a box of red wine on the counter,
some glasses. On a warm spring day like this,

I'll take the kids outside to play in his creek,
catch minnows and crayfish, till the pizza comes.
If not, he'll likely come to our place soon . . .

The world is never so much with us as when
it's gone. I stare at the screen, fingers on trackpad,
zooming and panning through the diorama.
No matter the angle, my father's looking away.
Now I become the car with its high-tech rig
of cameras: I approach, and slowly pass,
and all the while the man stands facing the oak,
as if he had some news to tell it—perhaps
those letters in his hand are some top-secret
summons or message it's his job to deliver?
And so he's Gabriel again, a messenger,
white dogwood blooms instead of a lily stalk,
the iconography clear, except: he's old,
he has no wings, there is no Mary here.

It took one year for the cancer to do its job,
a year in which I saw him almost daily.
I like to think he had important things
he could have told me had he chosen to.
Or was it up to me to ask some question?
Instead of asking, I fenced his yard with cedar
for his old dog. Instead of telling, he
turned on the television so we could watch
John Wick, the Spurs. So much time together,
so little said about the things that matter.
(I haven't started going through his papers;
perhaps the important messages are there.)

GEOFFREY BROCK

It was as if his back, I think, had always
been turned. With every click I half expect
the man on the screen to look, at last, toward me,
who longs to see his face, who dreads the smear.

SEASONAL CASES

Spring Vocative

Bursting bark-shell
jade-beaked bud

October is far still
hatch while you can

feed now
on the sun's milk

the wood's blood:
green me toward feel

Summer Ablative

The parched pasture
passing my window

isn't empty
the shadow cast

by the lone willow
isn't shadow merely:

a herd of black cattle
has pooled there

like ink in a bottle
has remade for itself

out of the glare
a deeper shade

GEOFFREY BROCK

Autumn Instrumental

The fuzzy hum
of bike tires on asphalt

drowning the hum
of thought at bay

the warm hum
of muscle on shinbone

of sun sinking in pinewoods
wind humming

with woodsmoke and resin
as songbirds give way

to crickets that hum
an understory

where nothing
knows or needs the words

Winter Genitive

The lone cardinal
perched on its branch

like the last red
leaf of the year:

my father watching
from his screen porch

heart still chirping
high in its tree

SPRING HAVING COME

after Paolo Febbraro's "Fiaba e morale"

He fell and died, the skier,
high up there in the snow.
And now, spring having come,

his son sets out from his home,
dark in the valley, to throw
a hook in the heavy river.

GEOFFREY BROCK

THE VAIN SUMMER

after Carlo Betocchi's "D'estate"

And it grows, the vain
summer,
even for me with my
thinning hair and gray sins:

behold the sly guest,
the wind,
as he stirs up grief
among magnolia branches

and hums his immodest
tune into
the ear of every leaf—
and then is gone,

leaving the leaves
still there,
the tree still green, but breaking
the heart of the air.

BETRAYAL

There was betrayal, father, when you broke
the pact we'd sealed one evening with two snuffed
cigarettes: that neither of us would smoke
again if the other didn't. But why am I left
tonight—though thirty years have passed and death
has stretchered you, gasping for air, away—
dwelling again on that day,
your voice, your breath,
as you (lost in the rush
of a fresh crush)
tell me your latest news . . . The reek
of you a proof, I thought, of weakness
of love. I'd wanted you to save me, father,
by saving yourself—for us to save each other.
That you couldn't, or wouldn't,
was something I didn't
want ever to have learned,
a truth that burned
down the throat of my lives,
back, toward my birth,
and forth, toward future children, future wives . . .

THE BALLAD OF JOHN-JACK

A boy by the roadside
hollered at me.
Stranger! he hollered,
hey stranger! said he,

if you're off to the city
and you meet a John-Jack
please tell him his son needs
him to come back.

Well finally I got there.
I'd promised the son
but I found a war raging
and was handed a gun,

and I fought for that city
and hated some other,
and the border kept shifting,
and brother killed brother,

till one day it ended
and I remembered again
the promise I'd made once
to look for a man.

So I looked and kept looking.
It took over my life.
It cost me some day jobs.
It cost me one wife.

I found him one morning
under a stone.
John-Jack had perished
of old age, alone,

and I groaned, and I wavered,
for I knew I should go
back to my hometown
to let his boy know.

I doubted I'd make it.
When somehow I did
I announced I was looking
for John-Jack's kid.

If you mean my daddy,
a young man replied,
I'm sorry to tell you
you missed him—he died.

He died by the roadside
a-waitin' for you.
You must be grandpa.
I've waited too.

Well I grieved like a father
who's just lost a son,
or an old man who longs for
but doesn't have one,

and I said to that fellow
I've finally come back,

GEOFFREY BROCK

and yes, I'm your grandpa.
My name is John-Jack.

So you left your family
to travel the world
and now that you're feeble,
white-haired and old,

you limp back to see 'em?
So be it, he said.
Take hold of my elbow.
I held, and he led.

DENTAL HYGIENE
THROUGH THE AGES

When I was a child
I brushed as a child

which is to say often
I didn't at all

but when I was a child
I was sharp of wit

and when omitting the brushing
I wetted the bristles

for I knew that my parents
vetted the bristles

*

Now I am a man
I brush as a man

which is to say thoroughly
to stave off rot

but now as a man
I am duller of wit

did I brush already
or not I forget

and no one to vet
these bristles but me

GEOFFREY BROCK

THE MAKERS

The children are the makers of the parents,
by cut and paste, by drag and drop, by trial
and terror. Out of a drawer of craft supplies
come monsters and self-portraits, come blue torrents
descending from gray cliffs and pooling while
glue dries on cotton clouds. Beneath such skies,

two larger figures stand beside two smaller
against a field of green, hands fused, heads sprouting
sunflower petals. A trail of seeds (or breadcrumbs?)
leads to the right, toward forests of no color.
And not till sun turns into moon and the trotting
cow in the pasture on the left becomes

these burgers on the grill do lullabies
get sung, their black notes weaving up like bats
to fashion night. And not till children sleep
does a house grow up around them, swelling in size,
filling with windows made of scissored bits
of landscape, in which yellowhammers keep

tacking the lawn in place. Then yellow buses
appear and children vanish, leaving their art
unfinished. And not until they too are grown
and shrinking slowly as mortgage balances
to fit new parts they'll never learn by heart
may children lay their parent bodies down.

II

THE SHINGLE STREET SHELL LINE

From the few human
        dwellings it reaches
(like the light-starved

        tentacle of a blind
deep-sea creature)
        over the shingle

beach toward a sea that,
        wave after wave,
reaches relentlessly

        back. Decades ago,
Meg now explains
        as we all step across it,

two women, old friends
        who were living through cancer,
placed the bleached shells

        of twenty-some thousand
whelks in a line
        three hundred yards long . . .

And now, as we crunch
        north up the shore
on our afternoon walk,

        my wife and I pocket
white whelks by the dozen—
        each tide leaves a crop

in its wake like a tithe—
          so that soon, when we come
crunching back down,

          we too can add,
as others have done,
          as others will do,

our shells to the line.
          (In a time-lapse,
the tentacle quivers

          as it frays in the elements
and is tidied by hands:
          now blurry, now sharper,

as if moving beneath
          a sheet of dark water.)
Meanwhile, beside us,

          the dark sea is breathing
calmly, some seals
          loll on a sand bar,

and much farther out,
          making for Felixstowe,
a motionless row

          of container ships pins
the horizon briefly
          in place, in time . . .

Beyond them, you
          can just make out
(if you have better eyes

       GEOFFREY BROCK

than our son, who squints
through his glasses in vain
before borrowing Paul's

binoculars), the ghostly
turbines that body
forth from the mist

to proclaim themselves
the forests of our future,
then sink back again

into the unseen,
there to go on
farming the wind

for power. The same
wind that's now rising,
blowing our daughter's

hair into the air
like a dark aura
as she swivels her phone

away from the sea
toward an old pillbox
still lodged in the dike

(*click*) and then (*click*)
a centuries-old
Martello Tower—

traces of different
wars, the same fears.
The sea, of course,

is rising too,
  as it did when the place
called Doggerland—ancient

  plains that once stretched
between Holland and here—
  drowned in these waters.

(In a time-lapse,
  the plains turn to islands
that shrink and are gone,

  .and the waters become
the Mare Germanicum,
  the Frisian the West the

North Sea, and we
  become and are captured
here for a frame—

  Ravi and Mira,
Padma and me . . .)
  Look.at us looking,

eyes to our lenses,
  taking small keepsakes,
leaving small traces;

  blink and you'll miss us.

GEOFFREY BROCK

LOSING A STARING CONTEST

for my daughter, at four

Sometimes when the steady
stream of her chatter dips

quietly underground
and all her galloping vim returns

to the trough of her body to feed,
I too become still, tethered

to the fixed brown of her eyes,
which, though the rest of her seems

keen to disown the daily
hand-me-downs of itself,

are already the size they'll be
when she is grown, and flaring in them

I see, as if projected on a wall
by the light of a match, the shadow

of the creature she will be
in time, when, with luck, I

will be old, but not gone—
and all the while, of course,

as if this were a game, she
is staring back at me

with a gaze of her own, seeing
what? But here the field of my vision

bleaches to white, as if I'd
stared at the sun, and my eyes

shut, and I hear her
snort and gallop away.

GEOFFREY BROCK

FOR MY SON AS HE SETS OUT

after Attilio Bertolucci's "Papavero"

This is a year of irises: our yard
was brimming with them as spring burned
off like fog and summer returned—
a sweet dark wine that made me drunk.

From clouds of mulberries to grains to grasses
ripeness was all, in the fitting
heat, in the slow drowsiness spreading
through the universe of green.

My life half over I watched our grown son
set out alone and vanish from sight
beyond the prison the flight
of the nighthawk makes in the spent

glow of a stormy evening. May this pain
give way humanely to that light
coming on inside the house for another meal
in air made cooler by hail

letting off steam in the distance.

AFTER MY FATHER: A CENTO

I learned to translate
                   where snowmen tame wild country.
They'll stand all night in snow.
                         I heard them singing—
I try to think of you and think of these—
singing "Our Father," voices older than speech,
whispering our gospels and histories,
translating us again into transparent tongues.

I can teach you how to translate: begin
bearing your son in your arms, our sons to us,
our congealed bodies waiting
                       without a tongue.
You, who leave us tongueless, with one eye,
I try to think of you and think of these.

Without a tongue,
                I had no way to translate—
none of us had fathers who knew that trick.
Instead
          I listen, my whole body a tongue.
As I learn infinitives, idioms, the grammar,
I mold desire into sentences, like maned sheaves,
to show us what your words had always meant.
I try to think of you and think of these.

I tried to say, "The horror is all yours,"
in its language of pure opacity
                     (*pait*   *paitpait*),

                                           GEOFFREY BROCK

like your tongue, breathing as quickly as you breathe.
But I cannot clearly remember you.

I listen for a dissonant singer in old oaks.
From a ravenous cavity, the voices of rasping tongues:
"Branches increase the acorn." I'll try to translate
the country of my origin

                to our sons.

There are things I fear. Translation, for example.
Evidence, lost tongues,

                   the disease of birth.
I try to think of you and think of these.
The terror is the getting lost in earth—
your son still trembles from your trembling.
The new snow on the ground is very pure,
translating us again into transparent tongues.

Now what you don't say I must say for you.

TOTEM

Hatched from the wet egg of a sculptor's eye
a quarter century ago, it grips
its squat stump, wings outstretched as if to dry.
Its bones are wires, its plumage ragged strips

of pages torn from my father's books, drizzled
with inky paint, barnacled with gimcracks
(buttons and sequins, beads and hair), as if risen,
drenched, from lakes of metaphor and syntax.

Call it "Tired Anhinga." Or "Hideous Bird."
And call it mine: a death-gift from my father.
I hid it with his ashes when I heard
his voice begin to seep from every feather:

slurring disjointed lines from his saddest poems,
squawking of bodies changed into new forms.

ODE TO A PARAKEET
ON HAMPSTEAD HEATH

My sight blurs, and a jet-lagged torpor weighs
my eyelids down, as if my tea were steeping
in Lethean waters, or the gauze of haze
swathing the Heath were ether. I'd be sleeping
here on this public bench, to which I've trekked
(passing the nearby Keats House on the way)
to view the skyline of my new demesne,
but for your shriek that wrecked
the sylvan peace, making me slosh Earl Grey
and doing more to wake me than caffeine.

I've heard tales of your mythic forebears: pets
disowned amid the "parrot fever" scare,
African Queen props loosed from Isleworth sets,
that pair that Hendrix, high, set free in Mayfair . . .
Invasive pests? Or immigrant successes?
Whatever name you're called, you've made yourself
at home here in this land whose brightest locals
were once the London buses,
and now you pull me from the yawning gulf
of park-bench slumber with your bracing vocals:

lifting my gaze, I thrill to see you smear
gray skies with color. No one says you sing
melodiously, but if our eyes could hear
they'd call your chartreuse tremolo of wing
and the red, swooping high note of your bill

an aria di bravura sung above
this city's orchestra of muted tones.
Before I've seen my fill
you flit behind a beech tree's curtain of
dark green, to dream of lost subtropic zones . . .

And there the poet goes, projecting. I'm
the one, not you, who's new to the neighborhood,
who's left his native continent and clime
in search of—what? New habitats? More food?
Who knows. Not me. At home, I long to travel;
abroad, I soon feel out of place and yearn
(as you do not) for home. Though if you ask
what "home" means, I may cavil:
the word's a shibboleth, a song we learn
by rote, an absence in a painted mask—

or so I'll say. (Still: how I envy creatures
who live where they were born and come to love it,
not blindly, but because they know its nature's
a taproot to their own, and so to leave it
would feel like tearing a heart from a living chest.
A bird could spend its whole life on this Heath.
Why fly to Rome or to the Eiffel Tower
if you can make a nest
high in that beech as pageants pass beneath,
as Big Ben faintly tolls each short-lived hour?)

And yet it's what we'll try to make here: *home*.
A flat in Kentish Town, not far away;
our kids in local schools, learning to roam
before they've had a chance to learn to stay . . .

GEOFFREY BROCK

That shriek again! Like Keats, the nightingales
have left this hillside for a further hill;
fled is their song. But you, bright alien bird,
spawner of origin tales,
make music, too. Teach me, while I'm still
awake, some old-world air, some brave new word.

THE MAYFLY: MAY 12, 1864

Having risen from a branch of the Ni River
during a lull in the Battle of Spotsylvania,
she lit on the blue upper lip of a dead
Confederate corporal, weary. As Union troops

began their fifth assault on Laurel Hill
she began to molt, her cloudy wings
clearing with the weather, her spectral body
brightening and swelling, as if the life

spilling from the ephemeral creatures around her
were filling her. Soon, she rose again,
joining the sudden frenzied cloud of her kind
that congregated there above the creek's

fizzing waters, their wings ten thousand leaded
windows pierced by an angling evening sun.

GEOFFREY BROCK

MIDWINTER LETTER

Dear son of mine, dear daughter,
      the forecast called
for a fine evening, and we
did laugh at first, but then we bawled;
our wine turned into water.
      Portentously,

even the moon was torn
      that night by schism,
half dark, half bright, but I—
blinded by rare optimism
and drunk on common scorn—
      believed a lie,

or more than one, and had
      the two of you
believing too. I'm sorry.
We didn't know what not to do.
Our country had gone mad
      in a red flurry.

        *

It fell to my dying father
      to say something true,
(as if your mother and I
had been relieved of duty), to
steady us both, gather
      us in his eye,

which was calm, and had seen
　　　　assassinations,
wars and genocides,
lower- and upper-case depressions,
and most things in between—
　　　　and which abides

now, we must hope, in us.
　　　　"This is the way
America works," he told
your tearful mother as she lay
her head on his shoulder, his voice
　　　　cool but not cold.

　　　　　　　*

Detached despite attachment:
　　　　like the alien
who briefs the Counselors
in that sci-fi poem he loved by Hayden . . .
Perhaps he too was sent
　　　　to these our shores

from some counter-earth, obscured
　　　　by a wreath of moons,
and now has been recalled.
And maybe even now he croons
"The Fox" or "Yellow Bird"
　　　　to some space-child,

telling them tales till late
　　　　of a world fraught
with "rage and bleeding and frenzy."

　　　　　　　　　　GEOFFREY BROCK

Let's say that: it's a pretty thought
and as such counterweight
        to current trends.

                *

I watched you, near that end,
        sitting beside
his throne-like hospice bed.
Mira, you read him poems: a ride,
a fish, a western wind.
        Ravi, you read

also, but silently,
        to yourself, hidden
in distant inscapes, afraid
of being blown, or caught, or ridden.
He murmured Innisfree,
        the bee-loud glade

buzzing in his mind's ear.
        Oh paradox
on paradox. Oh little
boats with your engines and your oarlocks,
oh brilliant bilge: much here
        is beautiful.

                *

Even the moon, that night,
        was fifty-fifty.
The talking heads droned on,
their facts and faces all as shifty

as sand or water, or light
        when the good light's gone.

I'm trying to glimpse a future
        where fathers are better,
and countries. All I see
tonight are spacemen. But if this letter
should find you there, then picture
        a joyous me,

not this large child, grieving
        at three a.m.
for his earthbound father,
his failing country. No, not him;
he is a ghost. You're living—
        and must live further.

(2017)

III

VIEW FROM MY DESK

How me of him, I think, as I look up
to see my old dog running along
the shadow of a high branch

barking and now leaping hopefully up
toward the squirrel running along
the actual branch

WALKING THE CAT

Each night I take the old dog for a walk.
I put his harness on, attach the leash,
and when we step outside into the dark

we find the cat, a shadow in that dark,
awaiting us, as always. For her, no leash,
but still she'll orbit us loosely as we walk.

The dog and I will take the lit sidewalk,
each tethered to a body by a leash,
as she roams free, a little blot of dark

patching the fabric of the larger dark:
under a fence, through thickets any leash
would tangle in, culverts no man can walk . . .

I listen for her faint bell as we walk
and try to make my voice into a leash,
pull her with cryptic words out of the dark

for a brief touch, perhaps, before the dark
reclaims her. The old dog strains then on his leash.
Above us, the old moon on its nightly walk,
the belled stars chiming faintly in their dark.

AFTER TRILUSSA

in memory of Frederika Randall, who fell

One night, Old Turtle, out for a stroll,
ventured to cross the road.
She'd never heard the word "pothole."
Later, when Toad

hopped by and saw her upturned shell,
he couldn't help but rave:
"You fool, you fell
into your own grave—

soon dawn will come, and cars!"
"I know," said Turtle, eyeing the sky;
"but now I can die
having seen the stars."

PARABLE

The January sun calls me to take
the bike down from its winter hook, and soon

I'm sprinting through a cut-glass afternoon
north on the Greenway, past pasture and lake,

mile after windless mile. Pedaling fast,
I pity the weak, who struggle, as if uphill,

in the southbound lane. But when, in Bentonville,
I turn for home, I'm chastened by the blast

of tailwind—headwind now—that like a tide
has borne me. Slogging back, as if through sand,

I feel the absence of my father's hand,
huge on my back, as he taught me to ride:

I wobbled down Corrib Drive, the ice-cream truck
my goal, his arm my motor and my guide,

till, when I was no longer terrified,
I rode alone. Blind to my princeling luck,

I even dared to wander from his side
and stand apart, as I licked my dripping cone,

as if I'd come there solely on my own—
as if I felt not gratitude but pride.

GEOFFREY BROCK

POKER NIGHT

It was only because our hosts had changed the night from
        Saturday to Friday
that I was able to attend at all. And it was only because I
        was attending
that I decided, late in the day as I bicycled in spring-like
        February weather

home from Lake Fayetteville, to stop at the Dickson Street
        Liquor Store
for an offering. I resolved to choose well—our hosts were
        famous among us
for their libations—and as I browsed the upper shelves
        I found myself

reciting a sonnet about lower shelves: *Luck is something I*
        do not understand
is how it begins, and ends. No one complained. Because
        I did choose well,
I worried, as I ferried it homeward in my bicycle's aluminum
        bottle cage,

about its fragility: *clink, clank-clank*, it groused. After one
        especially shrill
complaint, caused by a frost-heave in the asphalt (courtesy of
        the cold snap
that immured us for a week in early January), I pulled to
        the curb

at Sutton and Washington, hoping to increase the smoothness
      of my ride
by releasing some air from the tires, which I had filled
      that morning
to increase my speed. *For every action*, etc. Kneeling,
      I unscrewed

the valve cap on the rear tire. Dusk was dimming the tree-
      lined streets.
It was only because I'd stopped, just there, just then,
      that I saw it:
a dog, striding purposefully up the sidewalk toward me.
      A large

black lab, unchaperoned, and seemingly unaware of me.
      As it neared,
I pressed the valve pin, causing air to hiss stridently out
      of my tire.
And because the dog did not acknowledge my presence
      even then

I found myself recalling the Hasidim I live among
      each summer
in Outremont: on evenings much like this one they dress
      in black,
the patriarchs in their cake-box fur hats, their wives
      in their wigs,

and they stride down Durocher toward houses of worship,
        looking
never at me but always at something far in the distance,
        infinitely
beyond me. As it reached me, the dog turned right
        onto Sutton,

still on the sidewalk, then vanished over a rise into
        the darkening
Arkansas Sabbath. Above me, a streetlamp flickered on,
        as if
to make me visible again. The bottle glinted. I was
        feeling lucky.

IN MEMORY

I'll die in Montreal in the wake of winter.
Outside my window, gouts of snow will topple
from the gaunt branches of my favorite maple
toward the dark street, where they will turn to water.

Brown little alps, heaved by the snowplows skyward
after some storm, will have begun declining,
exposing like fossils the buried cars. Deep cleaning
will need to be done, a city will need to be scoured . . .

I'll die in winter—ah, but for now it is summer:
the sidewalk chirps with children; my grimly formal
next-door neighbor, in the broad shade of his shtreimel,
is off to greet the Sabbath. (He'd look no grimmer,

I'd wager, were he trudging to the gallows.)
I'll die some other Friday, in thawing weather,
thinking, perhaps, as I am now, of my father
and his long loneliness, propped on thick pillows.

I'll die as the Hasidim, who wear like blazons
each difference from their neighbors who are sinful,
parade down Durocher in black—not mournful,
for what was I to them? Through all those seasons,

they never did acknowledge me (our manners
clashed like our clothing) when we passed on sidewalks:
they stared ahead; I smiled at wigs, at side-locks.
Yet let them figure, here in these lines, as mourners . . .

GEOFFREY BROCK

Geoffrey Brock, a native of Southern climes,
has died in a cold country, far from his people.
A minor poet, known among friends for his supple
use of outmoded forms and his quaint rhymes,

he leaves a wife and children who—and so on.
And now he's gone from Outremont forever.
Don't bother praying: he was no believer
and isn't bound for any heaven or Sion.

It's all the same to him if you wed his widow
and fill the vague depression left in his mattress
or flirt, at Figaro, with his favorite waitress.
Soon even in memory he will cast no shadow.

EATING EARLY CHERRIES
AND THINKING OF PAVESE

1.

He died in Turin in the summer. In summer,
Turin feels as large and bare
and resonant as an empty square.
Sky rinsed with milk, clear but not luminous.
A river that's wide and flat as any highway
but lends no cool, no moisture to the air.

None of his friends were there.
He chose, for his death, a day
(the 27th) like any other
in that torrid August. He chose a room
(346) in an anonymous hotel,
and packets (12) of sleeping powder
dissolved in a glass of water.

He wanted to die, there in his own city,
like a stranger.

2.

        Ten years before,
late one spring, early in the war,
he'd visit his friends Natalia and Leone
bearing fresh cherries.
They'd see him, from their window,
appear at the end of their street, striding their way

to talk about a book,
or the appalling news of the day,
chewing the fruit and, with a sidelong look,
firing each pit against the pitted wall.

He liked the early cherries, the small,
watery ones—he said they had the "sapore
di cielo." He'd pull them one at a time
from the pocket of his coat—
a gesture that seemed lavish and miserly at once—
to give his friends a chance
to taste them too. For the rest of her life, Natalia wrote,
whenever she ate an early cherry
she'd think of Cesare
and of the fall, that spring, of France.

3.

Numbers need no translation:
346, 12, 27.
As for "sapore di cielo,"
some render it as "taste of heaven"—
one can see why.

But have you eaten early cherries lately?
To me they taste like sky.

SO TELL ME . . .

I. How Did It All Begin?

Ma dimmi: al tempo d'i dolci sospiri,
a che e come concedette amore
che conosceste i dubbiosi disiri?
—*Inferno 5:118–120*

The book was old and we, of course, were young.
Its story had been written (and somehow
this seemed important) in a foreign tongue.

It's true, by the way: you may feel awful now,
but if you summon happy memories back
you'll feel worse still. But since you long to know:

One day we met to talk about the book,
which both of us had read. We were alone.
Discussing the kissing scene was all it took—

our will, by then, was something not our own,
climbing and changing us, as roses refashion
arbors, or notes blank staves, tone by sweet tone.

As for the book, that author of our passion,
we closed it then to make a free translation.

GEOFFREY BROCK

II. What Are You Waiting For?

Why bother, now, continuing to climb?
Let others climb, who have the energy.
I'll sit right here until I've served my time.

Between lost youth and far senility,
the cage-like silence of these middle ages.
If only I'd brought my fiddle for company.

Instead I recall old music, passages
scored in my brain . . . I close my eyes and sway,
hearing each string, feeling their varied gauges,

becoming them—till I am no longer player
but fiddle, instrument being tuned, shriven
of discord, readied for some bow to lay

its body down on mine. Ah, maybe even
I, then, will be translated into heaven.

III. Is Heaven Even Enough?

Ma dimmi: voi che siete qui felici,
disiderate voi più alto loco
per più vedere e per più farvi amici?
—*Paradiso 3:64–6*

My will, these days, is soothed by the caress
of Love's voice, which allows me to desire
exactly what I have—no more, no less.

For if the place I craved were any higher,
then my desire would fail to harmonize
with that high voice whose will has sung me here.

You'll hear, from me, no discontented sighs.
I long to sing my part in Love's chorale,
for Love has willed I won't live otherwise,

and Love's song brings, when I can hear at all,
this peace. Its lyrics are an ancient language,
arcane in meaning (in the original

one noun means *love as charity as longing*)—
but no one translates; you learn it in the singing.

GEOFFREY BROCK

ALTERATION FINDS

Delirium

after Rimbaud

How many hours I kept
that vigil by your side—
entire nights, eyes wide,
excluded as you slept.

What I was wondering:
why you yearned to evade
the real. No one has prayed
harder for anything.

It wasn't for your life
I feared, but for mankind.
Did you, in the end, find
secrets for *changing life*?

Defaced

after Rilke

The head we cannot know,
nor its bright fruit, the eyes.
And yet the body has
its gaze: a lamp turned low.

Or else the breast would cease
to dazzle, the hips fail
to curve into that smile
that begets more than a kiss.

And flesh would lose all life,
not flare till there's no blind
it can't see *you* behind—
you, who must change your life.

Denial

after Seferis

The afternoon grew hotter
along our secret shore.
We thirsted in the glare
but couldn't drink the water.

On golden sand we traced
your name beside the sea.
The wind came like a sigh;
our writing was erased.

How passionate our life,
how full of sex and song,
spirit and heart—how wrong!
And so we changed our life.

GRAY COMMUNION

I still have conversations with my father.
Sometimes we're at the bottom of the ocean
and he's distracted by the lack of air.
It's hard to stay on topic when you're busy
turning the water into oxygen,
or trying to. It's also hard down there
to hear with any clarity. It's easy
if not quite fair to blame it on the weather.

Sometimes he's standing at a teller's window
with me on his shoulders. Some egregious fault
of hers has made him livid. He wants to close
all his accounts—he claims that he has many.
There is no oxygen inside the vault,
I whisper to him. What I mean is money.
Wounded, he shrinks beneath me. Says he knows.
But says the teller looks like his ex-widow.

Sometimes we're in his dirty living room
watching the Spurs, speaking chiefly in stats.
(He moved to San Antonio for a woman
who saved him, for a year or so. I have here
his gray communion document, which states
whoever eats this bread will live forever.
I can't imagine a more awful omen.
Naturally she and God lost faith in him;

he never spoke of it, but so I gather.)
Last night we dined on a terrace by a lake.

His breathing tubes kept slipping toward his mouth,
hindering meal and colloquy alike.
He tore them off and flung them down the stairs.
After supper, we argued over stars,
both of us smoking again, as in our youth.
I still have conversations with my father.

THE FIELD

As the plane drops beneath clouds I look out over the wing and
     see them again,
the parceled hills of home: twined with roads, ribboned
     with rivers.
No plot like its neighbor, none flat or square, all pieced into
     hill and swale

and dotted with stock ponds and clusters of trees I can't name
     from here.
There an amber field. There a green one, peppered with what
turn out to be cows. There a field of darker green. Soon
     I'm driving

between greens, blowing past an old man, perched on a
     John Deere,
pulling a yellow and red haybine through the alfalfa. It's
     mid-May,
the first cutting. It's hot and dry. Tomorrow he'll ted it,
     I think,

the next day rake it in windrows, and the next, if the
     weather holds,
roll up some bales. Maybe the bales will feed the cows
     across the road,
I think. Maybe, if the weather holds, I'll mow the grass
     this weekend

GEOFFREY BROCK

and finally finish painting the fence. Or maybe I'll just lie in
        the hammock,
in hackberry shade, beside the unfinished fence, staring up
the gray trunk with its long scar where, a few winters ago,
        an ice storm

tore off a huge branch. The mind wanders. What does it mean
        to waste
your life? Is it failing to feed something else? I brake at
        a crossroads
as a semi passes in front of me, pulling a trailer of chickens,
        their smell

seeping in through my vents. Why did the ten thousand
        chickens
cross the road? And which came first, the chicken or the
appetite for chicken? When I was a boy, I lived in a suburb

that had been carved like a bright cut of meat out of
        the countryside.
Behind our house, the last few acres of woods, and
        beyond them,
exploring one day, I found a large field, fenced with
        barbed wire,

and next to the fence, like a sentry, in the shade of a
        gray-bearded oak,
a huge bull with huge horns. He sized me up slowly,
then gazed back at the ground. The oak's trunk was
        on my side,

and I climbed it, then shimmied along a thick branch
        that stretched
like a catwalk over the field. I was not a fearless child,
yet there I was, suspended over bone-white horns,
        thinking myself

still safe in the forest. Or was I, I suddenly worried, now
in the field? A trespasser? The bull shrugged. And then
he was whispering something; it sounded like *I'm lonely*.

And suddenly I was lonely, and longed to be home,
and tried to scoot backwards, but back was too hard—
and now I was frightened and saw myself falling

and those horns like a hayfork spearing and tossing me
easily into the air, as bulls did to men on TV. Eyes closed,
I bear-hugged my branch and cried out for help. None came.

The plain fear of that moment dogged me for months, even
after we moved. Both forest and field are long gone,
carved into more suburbs, more neatly packaged

messy lives. But that bull is still vivid before me,
and sometimes, when I listen, he says things.
I am not meat, he whispers today. *I am a maker. I am—*

A van is honking behind me. I'm idling at a green light,
downtown. I press on the gas, and the blocked stream
of cars and of commerce resumes its urgent flow.

GEOFFREY BROCK

ON WHAT WOULD HAVE BEEN
MY FATHER'S 90TH BIRTHDAY

I sat beside the blazing Halloween bonfire, drinking
with friends, not thinking
of you, till the flames spat out an ember
that burned a pea-sized hole in my coat—my cue to remember
the story of your childhood scar:
how a coal launched from a glowing bar
lodged in your pants-leg, which was cuffed.
You couldn't find it, assumed it had been snuffed,
but it brooded there, until its bloom
brightened that grim Depression-era room
and began, as your widowed mother screamed, to climb.
It left an egg-shaped scar, which grew over time
as you did: hairless as plastic, so wide
I could fit my whole splayed hand inside,
until my hand, too,
over time, grew . . .

Then it was as if I had awoken
from my childhood, as if an eggshell around me had broken
and I was born into a grave new world where smoke
rose thick and orange as a runny yolk
from a fire out of which you seemed also to rise, as if to remind
me to remember you. And I blinked to find
my friends around me again,
and they listened as I tried, poorly, to explain.
Then all of us were quiet for a time, thinking,

and then someone raised a glass to you, to toast
your Halloween ghost,
and we resumed our drinking.

AFTERTHOUGHTS

The title of this book is meant in two ways. A number of the poems were written after, and in response to, the death of my father, the poet Van K. Brock (Oct. 31, 1932–Mar. 1, 2017). Some of those poems, and many of the others, are also in some way "after"—as in, in the manner of—other poems or works of art. Such texts are often called "imitations" and have long been seen as, in Samuel Johnson's words, "a kind of middle composition between translation and original design." They may also be called versions, or adaptations, or free translations—though my favorite term might be the one Donald Justice coined as the title of his 1973 collection, *Departures*. I've been writing and translating poems for forty years now, and the longer I do so the more compelling I find this middle ground, which I think of as a conversational space. It's also a space that complicates our derivative, Romantic notions of originality, which Goethe famously challenged:

> People always talk about originality, but what does it mean! As soon as we're born, the world starts acting on us, and keeps on to the end . . . If I could account for all I owe to great predecessors and contemporaries, little would remain.

All poets, Goethe suggests, are inescapably indebted to other poets, much as each of us is indebted to the people who raised us. But the word "after" usually signals a particular debt and a desire to acknowledge it. It's impossible, of course, to account for all such debts, but I have tried—in the interest, above all, of conversation—to acknowledge as many as I can, either in epigraphs or here below:

"The Day" has Horace in mind.

In "~~Annunciation~~," the painting I had in mind was Simone Martini's *Annunciation with St. Margaret and St. Ansanus.*

"Seasonal Cases" is after William Bronk's "Winter Vocative."

"Betrayal" takes its form and theme from Robert Lowell's "Rebellion."

"The Makers" is after Heather McHugh's poem "Fable."

"The Shingle Street Shell Line" was inspired by the earthwork sculpture of the same name by Lida Cardozo Kindersley and Els Bottema. It is dedicated to Meg Rosoff and Paul Hamlyn.

"After My Father: A Cento" consists of lines from the following poems by my father, in this order: "My South, My Russia," "An Absurd Snowman," "Efficiency Award," "Dream with Saints and Apples," "For One Who Is," "Island of Paradise," "Epistle to the Cicadas," "Epistle to the Cicadas," "My South, My Russia," "An Absurd Snowman," "Dream with Saints and Apples," "Book of the Dead," "Litany," "For One Who Is," "Book of the Dead," "Book of the Dead," "Dragging the Pond," "Childhood," "Land of the Old Fields," "Becoming a Child Again," "Ming Tapestry," "Peter's Complaint," "For One Who Is," "Departure," "Book of the Dead," "The Ivory-Billed Woodpecker," "Snake," "Peter's Complaint," "Ossabaw

Tabby," "The Nightmare: Ruth," "The Tree," "Land of the
Old Fields," "An Absurd Snowman," "To Flavia," "Land of the
Old Fields," "Elegy," "For One Who Is," "Departure," "Let-
ter," "Die Briefe (The Letters)," "Epistle to the Cicadas," and
"Letter." (NB: "Letter" is my father's translation of "Lettera" by
Franco Fortini.)

"Totem" is an imitation of the first section of Seamus Heaney's
"Clearances." The anhinga sculpture it describes (which is not
actually hideous) is by the Tallahassee artist Linda Hall.

"Ode to a Parakeet on Hampstead Heath" is of course a
response to Keats' "Ode to a Nightingale." It is dedicated to
Christian Wiman.

"The Mayfly: May 12, 1864" is after Miroslav Holub's "Mou-
cha" ("Fly").

"Midwinter Letter" takes its form from Hayden Carruth's
"Midsummer Letter" and bits of language from Robert
Hayden, W.B. Yeats, and Elizabeth Bishop.

"View from My Desk" was inspired by Don Paterson's "The
Handspring."

"After Trilussa" is a free translation of Trilussa's "La tartaruga"
("The Turtle").

"Poker Night" was inspired by the prose of Lydia Davis and is
dedicated to Martin Miller and Lisa Margulis.

"In Memory" is after Swiss poet Henry Spiess's "Je mour-
rai . . . ," which was also the model for Kostas Ouránis's "Θα
πεθάνω ένα πένθιμο του φθινόπωρου δείλι" ("I shall die one
gloomy autumn evening" in A.E. Stallings' translation) and,
most famously, César Vallejo's "Piedra negra sobre una piedra

blanca" ("Black Stone on a White Stone"). The latter was, in turn, the model for Donald Justice's "Variations on a Text by Vallejo" and hundreds of other imitations in various languages.

"Eating Early Cherries and Thinking of Pavese" incorporates translated bits of "Ritratto di un amico," Natalia Ginzburg's essay about Cesare Pavese.

"So Tell Me . . ." adapts three passages from the *Commedia* and is dedicated to Moira Egan and Damiano Abeni.

The three sections of "Alteration Finds" are free translations of, respectively, a passage from the "Délires" section of Rimbaud's *Une saison en enfer* (*A Season in Hell*), Rilke's sonnet "Archäischer Torso Apollos" ("Archaic Torso of Apollo"), and Seferis's poem "Ἄρνηση" ("Denial").

Each stanza of "Gray Communion" borrows a line from a poem by my father or, in the case of the third stanza, from his communion certificate: "turning the water into oxygen" (from "Leaving Camp"), "There is no oxygen inside the vault" (from "Ghost Town"), "whoever eats this bread will live forever" (John 6:51), and "After supper, we argued over stars" (from "Peter's Complaint").

"The Field" was inspired by Jennifer Grotz's poem "The Forest," and both poems are in conversation with Randall Jarrell's poem "Field and Forest." It also has in mind James Wright's "Lying in a Hammock at William Duffy's Farm in Pine Island, Minnesota," my father's "The View from My Hammock," Cesare Pavese's "The Boy Who Was in Me," and Anthony Hecht's "A Hill."

ACKNOWLEDGMENTS

I also owe debts of gratitude to the editors of the following publications in which versions of the following poems first appeared:

32 Poems: "~~Annunciation~~"

Copper Nickel: "In Memory," "The Makers," "Parable"

The Cortland Review: "Autumn Instrumental" (as "Evening Song: St. Marks Trail")

Divining Dante: "So Tell Me . . ."

Ecotone: "Forces of Nature," "Walking the Cat"

Electronic Poetry Review: "Spring Vocative"

Literary Imagination: "The Field," "Poker Night"

Literary Matters: "Eating Early Cherries and Thinking of Pavese," "Street View (A Visitation)," "Losing a Staring Contest," "Betrayal," "The Shingle Street Shell Line"

The Literary Review: "Totem"

The London Magazine: "On What Would Have Been My Father's 90th Birthday," "View from My Desk," "Ode to a Parakeet on Hampstead Heath"

Massachusetts Review: "The Mayfly"

Michigan Quarterly Review: "After My Father: A Cento" (as "A Cento for My Father"), "Gray Communion"

The New Criterion: "Summer Ablative" (as "Drive")

Paris Review: "Dental Hygiene Through the Ages"

Poetry: "Alteration Finds," "The Day," "Watching My Son Set Out" (as "Poppies"), "The Vain Summer" (as "Summer"), "Spring Having Come" (as "Fable and Moral")

Yale Review: "Midwinter Letter"

Finally, I'm grateful as well to friends who read some or all of these poems and offered help or encouragement: Andrea Cohen, Boris Dralyuk, John DuVal, Moira Egan, Paolo Febbraro, Jennifer Grotz, Randall Mann, Andrew Shields, Sidney Wade, Rosanna Warren, and Christian Wiman. And above all to my first and last reader, Padma Viswanathan.

Geoffrey Brock is an American poet and translator. He is the author of two previous collections, *Weighing Light* and *Voices Bright Flags*; the editor of *The FSG Book of Twentieth-Century Italian Poetry*; and the translator of various books of poetry, prose, and comics, mostly from Italian. His poems have appeared in journals including *Poetry* magazine, *Paris Review*, *Yale Review*, and *Best American Poetry*, and he has translated authors including Patrizia Cavalli, Cesare Pavese, and Giuseppe Ungaretti. His translations have received ALTA's National Translation Award for Poetry and the PEN Center USA Translation Prize, among others. Brock is a Distinguished Professor of English at the University of Arkansas and the founding editor of the *Arkansas International*.